ABAYOMI
THE BRAZILIAN PUMA

Darcy Pattison

Kitty Harvill

The True Story of an Orphaned Cub

Abayomi, the Brazilian Puma:
The True Story of an Orphaned Cub

ePub ISBN: 978-1-62944-002-6
Library Paperback ISBN: 978-1-49520-240-7
Paperback ISBN: 978-1-62944-001-9
Hardcover ISBN: 978-1-62944-000-2

Library of Congress Control Number:
2013919505

Mims House
1309 S. Broadway
Little Rock, AR 72202
http://mimshouse.com

Kitty Harvill
Dedicated, with Love, to the memory of my own "little puma," Rocky - my muse, my inspiration and my companion.

Darcy Pattison
Always, for Dwight.

Acknowledgments

Thanks to Márcia Gonçalves Rodrigues, PhD, Environmental Analyst of ICMBio/MMA (Ministry of the Environment) and Sérgio A. P. Ferreira, IT-System Analyst and Wildlife Monitoring Expert of Puma Corridor; Marco Antônio Cintra Pacheco, Biologist of Puma Corridor; Jorge Aparecido Salomão Jr, Veterinary of Puma Corridor; Marcelo de Queiroz Telles Veterinary of Paulína Zoo; Peter Crawshaw Jr, Ph.D. and Environmental Military Police of Campinas.

And to make possible Abayomi's chance to go back to wildlife: Galvão Engenharia S.A., Melina Vieira Coura, Mauricio Pinheiro Gutemberg Guerra , and Fabio Leite de Moraes; NEX Santa Rosa; Brazilian Sugar Cane Industry Association (UNICA), Garnero Family, Forum das Américas, United Nations Association-Brazil (UNAB) and Fazenda Talisman.

We also thank Harvill's husband, Christoph Hrdina, co-founder and board member of Funatura, Foundation for Nature, and board member of Society for Wildlife Research and Environmental Education(SPVS).

In the far south, in Brazil, a puma cub was born in the early spring month of October 2012. The cub and its mother lived too close to people, in sight of skyscrapers. It was a dangerous place to live.

Once deep forests covered this land. Then people came and built villages that grew to large cities that crowded out the wild pumas.

Forests became orange, coffee or corn plantations. Recently, many of those have become sugar plantations, which were needed to make fuel for the many cars that zipped along the roads.

Here, the mother puma only walked abroad at night on silent paws.

Even farmers who had lived on the land for forty years had never seen her or her kin.

She was invisible.

Scientists realized that wild places were disappearing and started working to create corridors. Like a hallway from one room to another, the corridors were trails for wild creatures to travel from one wild place to another wild place.

Now, though, there are few wild places left, few safe places. Some pumas have no choice: they must live too close to man.

In Brazil, pumas hunt and eat armadillos, capybaras, or white-ringed coatis. But sometimes, it is hard to hunt.

In early November 2012, the mother puma found easy prey: chickens.
And the chicken farmer was mad.
He decided to set a trap and find out what sort of creature was eating his hens.

That very night, November 26, the mother puma probably left her cub in the middle of the sugar cane fields so she could hunt for his supper.

Suddenly, at 2:15 a.m., on
November 27, she was caught
in the chicken coop trap.
Then everything went wrong.

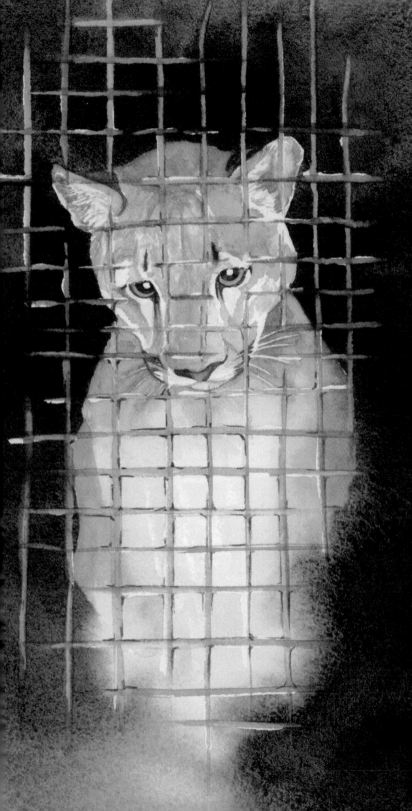

The officials who arrived first couldn't find a veterinarian, the only officials who could use a tranquilizer gun. It was hard to wait and wait. So, a fireman and the chicken farmer tried to force the mother puma into a cage.

She fought back.

Once, she hit her head hard against the side of the cage and was dazed.

After hours of struggling, she died.

When the puma scientists finally came, they examined the dead puma and realized that she was a nursing mother.

Where were her cubs?

How could they survive without their mother?

Wildlife officials followed the mother puma's footprints.

They searched the sugar cane fields.

No cub.
Then, a heavy rain washed away all
traces of the mother puma's trail.

If there were cubs, the officials
couldn't find them.
They were invisible.

How does a puma cub survive
without his mother?
He must hunt.
Maybe small birds.
Maybe a baby rodent.
Small teeth and claws.
Baby leaps and tiny growls.
Alone.
Invisible.

On December 19, twenty-three days later, at a farm a mile away from the chicken coop, dogs cornered the cub. He was scrawny and dehydrated, staggering around in a pasture next to a wooded area.

This time, wildlife officers safely captured the cub. Later, DNA tests confirmed this cub belonged to the mother puma killed at the chicken coop. He was named Abayomi, which in the Tupi-Guarani native language means "happy meeting."

It was a happy meeting that scientists had found Abayomi alive. Without his mother, Abayomi must live for a time behind a fence.

But the scientists knew that Abayomi belonged to the wild. Abayomi could not know his food came from the scientists.

He could not learn the way they looked.
He could not learn the way they moved.
He could not learn the way they smelled.
He could never be petted by a human hand.
And, while Abayomi learned the ways of the wild, the scientists must be invisible.

And if the scientists could stay invisible, there would come a day when Abayomi would return to the wild.

There would come a day when Abayomi—like his mother before him—only walked abroad at night on silent paws...

. . . wild and invisible.

FACTS ABOUT ABAYOMI

Puma, *Puma concolor*

The puma is sometimes called a cougar, mountain lion, or a panther. They are the second heaviest cats in the Western Hemisphere behind the jaguar. Traditionally, pumas had the largest geographic range of any land or terrestrial mammal in the Western Hemisphere. They are found from Canada through the United States, Central and South America to the tip of Chile. However, the puma is no longer found in the eastern United States, except for the endangered Florida puma. Some estimate there are only 150-200 Florida pumas left in the wild, up from just 20 in the 1970s. In the western United States, the population remains small but stable.

It is important to maintain pumas population in this region of Brazil because pumas helps to keep under control the capybaras population, which carry ticks that can transmit Brazilian tick fever (similar to the U.S. Rocky Mountain spotted fever) to humans.

Born: October, 2012, near Campinas, São Paulo, Brazil
Captured on December 19, 2012
Release date: Late 2014 or early 2015

OUR URBAN WORLD

The World Health Organization* reported that in 2010 the world is now over half urban. For the first time in history, more than half the world's population lives in cities. 100 years ago, only 20% of the world's population lived in cities. In 1990, only 40% called a city a home. Some predict that by 2050, 70% of people will live in a city. As urban areas grow, the environmental question has changed. Now we must ask, "How can we share our world with wild creatures?"

(*http://www.who.int/gho/urban_health/situation_trends/urban_population_growth_text/en/)

CORRIDOR PROJECTS

Wildlife corridor projects connect wild places so that plant and animal species can travel between the wild places. This is important so that a species doesn't become inbred and lose genetic viability. There are corridor projects on every continent except Antarctica. Read more about Corridor Projects here:

Conservation Corridor: http://www.conservationcorridor.org/
This site has information on conservation and corridor science.

Florida Wildlife Corridor Project www.floridawildlifecorridor.org
Learn more about saving the Florida Panther.

Asian Nature Conservation Foundation (ANCF)/Asian Elephant Research and Conservation: www.asiannature.org
The ANCF has several Asian elephant corridor projects.

READ MORE:

Abayomi and the Brazilian Puma Corridor Project:
www.icmbio.gov.br/corredordasoncas
Learn more about pumas in South America and see photos from camera traps.

The Cougar Network: www.cougarnet.org
Learn more about pumas in North America through maps, videos and publications.

KITTY HARVILL

www.facebook.com/KittyHarvill

Kitty Harvill specializes in wildlife art, especially endangered species, and works in watercolor, pastel, oil and cut paper. She has a dual residency in Arkansas/U.S. and Brazil and is actively involved with the conservation efforts in southern Brazil. Recent titles include *Wisdom, the Midway Albatross* (Mims House), *Up, Up, Up! It's Apple-Picking Time* (Holiday House) and *Vida Livre* (published in Brazil). Born in Clarksville, Tennessee, Harvill holds degrees in painting and illustration.

DARCY PATTISON

www.darcypattison.com

Published in eight languages, Darcy Pattison's recent nature books include *Wisdom, the Midway Albatross* (Starred review in *Publisher's Weekly*, Mims House), *Desert Baths* (2013 NSTA Outstanding Science Trade Book, Sylvan Dell), and *Prairie Storms* (Sylvan Dell). Her books have been recognized for excellence by starred reviews in *Kirkus*, *BCCB*, and *PW*. She was the 2007 recipient of the Arkansas Governor's Arts Award, Individual Artist for her work in children's literature. She and her husband live in North Little Rock, AR.

CPSIA information can be obtained at www.ICGtesting.com
Printed in the USA
LVIW01n1612160315
430760LV00008B/17

9 781629 440002